Making Room for Jesus:

Getting Rid of Mental, Emotional, Spiritual, and Physical Clutter

Laura Baggett

ISBN: 1532841477
ISBN-13: 978-1532841477

To David – my best friend, my hero, my biggest fan, and the One God picked out for me.

CONTENTS

WHY I WROTE THIS BOOK

If your goal is to get organized, there are many books written by many authors with a plethora of methods – all guaranteed to help you. I've read several of them. One actually worked for me.

This book is not about *how* to declutter your house.

The method you choose is incidental. If it works for you, that's wonderful. What I want to address are the spiritual applications, implications, and lessons learned along the way. How you choose to purge your stuff is mostly a physical issue, but the decisions made in the process and the thoughts and emotions that will emerge... dealing with those is where the real life-change happens.

What motivates us to buy more than we need? Why do we have trouble letting go of things that no longer serve us? Is it simply a matter of American consumerism or something deeper?

Some – perhaps most – of the work of decluttering is mindless: toss the things that are broken or stained, donate the things that don't fit or aren't needed, and then find a place for what remains. This is pretty straightforward when we're dealing with the contents of a junk drawer or going through our spice rack. But what happens when we run across that baby blanket? What about that lamp that belonged to a seemingly unforgiveable relative? How do we stop berating ourselves for no longer fitting into our favorite jeans?

And what does all this have to do with our relationship with God?

That's what I want to explore in this book. Care to join me?

1 WHERE YOUR TREASURE IS

Do not lay up for yourselves treasures on earth, where moth and rust destroy and where thieves break in and steal, but lay up for yourselves treasures in heaven, where neither moth nor rust destroys and where thieves do not break in and steal. For where your treasure is, there your heart will be also.

Matthew 6: 19-21 English Standard Version

It all began with a movie. I watched *War Room* on a Saturday afternoon and came home determined to create my own little prayer closet where I could fight on behalf of my family. I knew just the right spot – a little closet under the staircase. Like most of my house, though, it was full of stuff. We had moved into the house two years prior, and inside were items that had no other home and boxes I hadn't been able to face opening because they were labeled with dreaded words like "Misc.," and "Laura's Desk." They contained a hodgepodge of items like pictures, papers, artwork from my children, and craft supplies bought with good intentions.

I had done my best to ignore the space for months and

months, but now it was time to dive in. Without actually sorting anything, I emptied the closet. Some of the things went out to the garage to join other similar boxes and piles. Other boxes found a new home in the corner of our school room. I was still avoiding dealing with the clutter itself, but at least I had an empty space. I found an old card table in the garage, an unopened tablecloth purchased for "the future," and a lamp that was sitting unused on top of a pile. And then I began to meet with the Lord in that space.

It quickly became my favorite place in the house. I was growing spiritually in my walk with Christ. The walls gradually held handwritten prayers and Bible verses I was memorizing. I noticed that, at the end of my time each morning, I would carefully stack the books I was using, not wanting anything to be out of place or to disturb the serenity of that spot. It was the only place in the house that only contained what was needed and loved. Nothing else was allowed in.

Four pieces of paper attached to the wall contained lists of things I was praying over for my husband, my two children, and myself. The ones for my husband and children had been easy to write. I could easily see areas in their lives where I needed God to work on their behalf. My own list took a lot longer to compose. Eventually, my list contained several categories, and one of those was "Home." In that section I listed:

- Getting rid of excess stuff
- Desire/plan for creating and maintaining order
- Atmosphere reflecting the fruits of the Spirit

I didn't know how to do any of those things on my own. I had tried and failed countless times. While I had been successful in many other areas of my life, my home taunted me as a failure. I desperately needed His help.

Sabbath Study
Not coincidentally (is anything with God ever

coincidental?), I began leading an online Bible study about this same time. We were studying *Breathe* by Priscilla Shirer. It was all about the principle of the Sabbath and how it applied to our everyday, modern lives. I've discovered recently that much of what I have been taught from the Old Testament is, at best, fragmented and incomplete. While I've always viewed that Fourth Commandment as a rule about what shouldn't be done on Sundays, it turns out that adding a burdensome rule was far from God's true intention.

God's people had been slaves in Egypt for 400 years. All they knew was working hard, endlessly. Rest was simply not a part of their experience. The Egyptian gods (and thus Pharaoh and everyone under his rule) demanded more and more from them. If they managed to meet one goal, another higher one was immediately set and the conditions made more and more difficult. While certainly many were still taught about the God of Abraham, Isaac, and Jacob, the only gods they experienced in their daily lives were demanding and impossible to satisfy.

Finally, through a series of miracles culminating in the Passover and crossing the Red Sea on dry land, the people were free. But as many of us have seen in our own lives, being physically free and being mentally, emotionally, and spiritually free are very different things. The people were free, but they were still acting and thinking like slaves. They needed a mindset change. They needed to understand the God they were following, how to relate to Him, and how to relate to one another. That's where the Ten Commandments come in.

The first four commandments are focused on showing the people who God is, how He is different from the gods of Egypt, and what He requires.

And God spoke all these words, saying, "I am the LORD your God, who brought you out of the land of Egypt, out of the house of slavery. [Identification] *You shall have no other gods before me.*

[They are to follow and serve Him only, not a bunch of different gods, all clamoring to be satisfied.] *You shall not make for yourself a carved image, or any likeness of anything that is in heaven above, or that is in the earth beneath, or that is in the water under the earth.* [He is not limited by the workings of human hands.] *You shall not bow down to them or serve them, for I the LORD your God am a jealous God, visiting the iniquity of the fathers on the children to the third and fourth generation of those who hate me, but showing steadfast love to thousands of those who love me and keep my commandments. You shall not take the name of the LORD your God in vain, for the LORD will not hold him guiltless who takes his name in vain.* [He is worthy of respect, and calling on Him is a serious matter. He actually hears and responds.] *Remember the Sabbath day, to keep it holy. Six days you shall labor, and do all your work, but the seventh day is a Sabbath to the LORD your God. On it you shall not do any work, you, or your son, or your daughter, your male servant, or your female servant, or your livestock, or the sojourner who is within your gates. For in six days the LORD made heaven and earth, the sea, and all that is in them, and rested on the seventh day. Therefore, the LORD blessed the Sabbath day and made it holy."* Exodus 20: 1 – 11

Just think about how radical of an idea the Sabbath would have been to the children of Israel. They knew no other existence than work – constant, mind- and body-breaking work. There was no rest in Egypt. The Egyptian gods and pharaohs and slave masters allowed no time for rest. In fact, the gods, Pharaohs, and masters hardly took any time for rest themselves.

And yet, this "new" God actually *commanded* them to rest.

Obedience on that first Sabbath after Mount Sinai would have taken quite a lot of courage. They would have had to overcome their fears of punishment. Also, they were in the desert away from the stored-up provisions of Egypt. How would they have enough to eat if they took a day off? Resting on the Sabbath required a huge amount of faith in this God they had heard about from their ancestors but were just beginning to know personally.

Making Room – Spiritually, Mentally, Emotionally, and Physically – for God

Similarly, stopping our compulsions to acquire and save – perhaps even hoard or at least stockpile – requires trusting that God will provide what we need. It requires resting. It requires change.

The Sabbath is not just about clearing our schedules for a day. It's about making a profound mindset change.

… the Sabbath principle is not limited to our calendars and schedules. It also applies to the spaces in which we live, work, and play. Our tendency toward too-full lives often expresses itself most tangibly in our over-crowded closets, unmanageable table surfaces, and cluttered desks as we cram them full of far more than we need. Even our children fall prey to the chaos of overcrowded living as their toy boxes and bookshelves overflow with more than they could ever manage. In the meantime, they sit, chin in hand, complaining of boredom. (Shirer, 2015)

When we get rid of our stuff, when we purge those things in our lives that are no longer useful or beneficial, we're not only making more room in our houses. We're making more room in our lives and hearts. In a very real way, we're making room – spiritually, mentally, emotionally, and even physically – for God. We're turning from a life of slavery to a life of freedom, and just like the children of Israel, we're going to need a new way of thinking.

Here's where this can get a bit tricky (for me, at least): these things, activities, and even people that are taking up so much room in our lives aren't necessarily inherently evil. It's comparatively easy to spot a sin issue and know that it has to be removed immediately (although the actual removal may still be quite challenging). But what if it's not really a sin issue? Is having too many sweaters in my closet a moral failing? Is holding on to books I've never read and don't really intend to read going to lead me down a path of sin and degradation? Probably not. As far as I can tell, there's nothing in Scripture that declares that owning too much stuff is sinful. There's also nothing declaring a Krispy Kreme doughnut to be evil, but there's a reason that gluttony is listed as one of the deadly sins. You can absolutely have too much of a good thing.

That's where Sabbath rest comes into play. It's about keeping life in its proper context. It's setting appropriate boundaries around good things so that we don't go back into slavery. It's about trusting in God's provision so that our blessings don't turn into burdens. The Sabbath is about surrendering my desire for more, more, more – even when what I'm pursuing isn't inherently evil.

Blessings from God come in all forms. Many are spiritual in nature and exist "in heavenly places" (Ephesians 1). Others are feelings and experiences, relationships, love, friendship, a sense of belonging, and so forth. But still others are physical objects: our homes, our vehicles, our clothes, our books, … our STUFF.

It's not possible to have too many spiritual blessings. And I've never known anyone to get overwhelmed by too much genuine, healthy love and friendship. But those physical blessings – those are the things that can begin to take over if we're not careful.

Blessings are meant to be enjoyed. They are demonstrations of God's love and care for us. Sometimes they are also challenging and designed to grow us in our faith. But I don't think they're ever meant to become burdens. Any time an object interferes with our ability or willingness to be or do what God has planned for us, something is amiss.

Are there items in your home that started out as blessings but have become burdens? Maybe it's not a particular item but the sheer number of them that is weighing you down. Is the volume of your possessions preventing you from following the Lord in any way? Do you feel enslaved to your home, your schedule, or any other aspect of your life? If so, what will be necessary to live in freedom?

2 DON'T BASE DECISIONS ON WHAT *MIGHT* HAPPEN

Therefore, do not be anxious, saying, "What shall we eat?" or "What shall we drink?" or "What shall we wear?" For the Gentiles seek after all these things, and your heavenly Father knows that you need them all. But seek first the kingdom of God and His righteousness, and all these things will be added to you.

Therefore, do not be anxious about tomorrow, for tomorrow will be anxious for itself. Sufficient for the day is its own trouble.
Matthew 6:31-34

Every item that we own is a result of a decision. We purchased the item because we believed it would serve some purpose in our lives. Maybe we needed it. Maybe we just thought it looked pretty. Maybe we wanted to impress someone else.

In other cases, the items may be in our homes as a result of someone else's decision. It might have been a gift. It might have been left by the previous owners of the house. It might belong to a roommate, child, or spouse.

Either way, a decision was made that resulted in each item entering the door. A decision will also have to be made in order for it to remain on, or leave, the premises. Actually two choices are necessary: (1) Am I going to keep it? And (2) If I'm going to keep it, where will it be stored?

This sounds simple enough, and for most of the things that are discovered during the decluttering process, it actually is simple. But then there are other things for which the answers just aren't immediately clear. Often what lies at the heart of these indecisions is a mixture of guilt, fear, and insecurity. In a strange twist, hope can even be a source of clutter. Hoping for things to be different in the future can cause us to store up far too many "just in case" and "I will need this when ..." objects.

But It Might Work in the Next House...

During our seventeen years of marriage, my husband and I have moved thirteen times. Newton's Third Law – a body in motion tends to stay in motion while a body at rest tends to stay at rest – is surprisingly true, not just physically but emotionally and mentally as well. While I know people who would never dream of moving away from their hometown, moving from place to place can become equally addictive. The idea of "settling down" can become simultaneously an idealized goal and a deep fear.

By the time this book is published, we will have lived in the same house for three years. That's a record amount of time for us. Not only are we still here, we're not even planning an upcoming move. With a 15-year mortgage, we've gone so far as to have aspirations of paying off the house!

I knew that moving-every-year-or-two had become a mindset over the years, but I saw it in a new way during the decluttering process. There were pictures, lamps, spare bedding, curtains – all sorts of home décor items – that had been moved from location to location in spite of their age. The reason? "It might work well in our next house."

Unless you are actually planning a move within the next year, please let go of items that you aren't currently using and that just don't "go" in your current home. If you don't like something enough to find a way to make it fit now, chances are good that you don't actually like it that much, and you wouldn't want to bring old, barely-tolerated items into a new space anyway. Instead, focus on surrounding yourself with the things that you really like. Go ahead and unpack the boxes, mentally as well as physically.

But It Might Fit Again Someday...

About a year after my first child was born, I joined Weight Watchers and got down to my lowest adult weight. During that time, I bought a pair of jeans that I loved. The size number on the tag was thrilling to me, and I really liked how they fit. Literally within a month of hitting my goal weight, I became pregnant with my daughter.

My daughter is now seven years old. Three of the above-mentioned moves have taken place since she was born, and every time, those blue jeans have been loaded up and brought to the next house. I thought that keeping them would motivate me. I thought, "Won't it be great to be able to put these on again?"

They didn't motivate. They discouraged. I finally let them go.

Ironically, since donating those jeans, I've lost a good bit of weight. I'm feeling good about myself again. But the scale shows a different number from that time. Also, a second pregnancy changed my body once again. Even if the scale reflected a return to that former state, my hips would protest at fitting into those jeans again. And besides, styles have changed quite a bit.

If you're holding on to some item of clothing because "it might fit again someday," ask yourself a few questions. Does seeing that item truly motivate you, or does it actually discourage you? Unless it provides tremendous, tangible motivation, let it go. Has your body changed in ways that even weight loss would not significantly alter? If the answer is "yes," embrace those changes, and let it go. If you saw that item at a store and it fit, would you buy it? If the answer is "no," let it go.

3 YOU CAN'T DECLUTTER FOR SOMEONE ELSE

If you're mad at your family, your room may be the cause.
- Marie Kondo, *The Life-Changing Magic of Tidying Up*

After I really got rolling with decluttering my house, I naturally wanted to start tackling areas that belonged to other people – specifically my children's rooms and my husband's closet. I tried various methods for getting my kids to part with stuff. I asked them nicely. I explained the myriad benefits of a more spacious room. In some less-than-shining moments, I may have even threatened to throw stuff away if they couldn't keep their rooms clean and organized.

At the end of the day, though, the only person whose attitude I could actually affect was my own, and for the change to be lasting, others would need to be intrinsically motivated to do it, not cajoled or harassed into it. Interestingly, the more progress I made in decluttering personally, the more interested they became. It began to spread through the family like some sort of Tidy Virus.

I had an audio version of the decluttering book I had

used, and my husband decided to listen on his morning walks. That, combined with seeing the difference it had made for me, convinced him to finally take the plunge. Not following "the rules" from the book, he decided to tackle the most enormous job in our home – the garage. It took several evenings and weekends, but many SUV-packed trips to the garbage dump and thrift store donation center later, we had finally reclaimed it. And yes, he eventually organized his closet as well.

Decluttering with Children

Once my children were on board, at least partially, we began going through their rooms. We started with clothes. They both brought every bit of clothing into the living room, each with their own huge pile. One item at a time, a decision was made: keep, donate, or toss. Unless an item was too worn out to donate, I let each of them make the choices. While one was more ruthless in culling than the other, eventually they had each cut down the amount they owned by at least a third.

Next we tackled their books. Since I had already sorted most of our books that were kept in another location, sorting through the books in their rooms was a pretty fast process. Again, I let them make the decisions, even when it meant parting with books that had more sentimental attachment for me than for them.

We got bogged down with my daughter's toys. When she was in the room with them, she couldn't bear to part with anything. Then we hit upon a plan. Since the goal was to focus on what she wanted to *keep* instead of on what she wanted to *toss*, I asked her – while we were in a completely different part of the house – to make a list of the items she wanted to keep. The list could be as long as she wanted, but it had to be from memory. In other words, the items had to matter enough that she could actually remember them. We then went into her room, got those items out, and brought them all into the living room.

The original plan was that my son and I would go through her room without her present and gather everything that remained into "donate" and "toss" bags and boxes in order to save her from any angst. In the end, though, she sat on her bed in the middle of the room and watched as we cleared out everything. She did ask for a couple of other items to stay, and we moved those to the living room with the other "keep" items, but surprisingly, there was very little that she wanted from what remained. I think she was just relieved to not have to go through the process by herself. The decisions had already been made in an emotion-free place.

Seeing her clean, empty space was transformational. We scrubbed the surfaces, vacuumed the carpet, and freshened the bed linens. It was a beautiful blank slate. Then as we brought the items from the living room back to her bedroom, she chose a location for everything. For the first time, everything in her room had a home.

The crib mattress

My son had never been a big "toy person," so that part wasn't a huge challenge for him. His biggest struggle was with sentimental items and memorabilia. He had trophies, tickets from multiple sporting events he attended, and various certificates and letters that were important to him. The trouble was that everything was scattered across the top of his dresser haphazardly. Eventually we settled on some suitable storage items to at least keep the surface a bit clearer.

What I most wanted him to part with was his old crib mattress. He had already been in a regular-sized bed for several years, but we still had his old mattress for times when he would sleep on the floor in his sister's room or vice-versa. Truthfully, the first time we had considered parting with it about a year earlier, I couldn't bring myself to do it. There were just too many memories attached. I was finally ready, though, but he wasn't. I tried all forms of bribery and logic, but they weren't working. He did not want to part with that thing, and I didn't have the heart to just grab it from him and force the issue. Plus, I had already figured out that forcing someone to declutter just doesn't work for a number of reasons. It was being kept under my bed, though, and I wanted it out of there. Eventually we compromised after discovering a just-right spot under his loft bed up against the wall. It may be there until he moves away to go to college, but at least it's out of the way.

Lead by Example Instead of by Prodding

As much as we may want to, we can't make decisions about what is important to someone else. Just as no one else might understand why I hold onto that 24-year-old dress in my closet, I can't understand why my husband is so attached to some of his things. Our emotions, our histories, our reasons ... they're all unique. And they should be respected.

I can't properly deal with someone else's clutter. The best approach is to focus on my own stuff and encourage anyone who wants to join me.

In the same way, I can't properly deal with someone else's sin. The best approach is for me to focus on my own relationship with the Lord and to encourage anyone who also wants to follow Him.

The quote at the beginning of this chapter ("If you're mad at your family, your room may be the cause.") made me laugh the first time I heard it. But then I realized how true a statement it really is. So often, when I'm angry or frustrated, it's not because of what someone else has done – at least not entirely. It's also because my own failures or perceived failures are being brought to light in some way. If we're running late, I may be outwardly angry at my children, but inwardly I'm berating myself for not being a better manager of my time. If the house is a mess, I may complain about tasks that others should have done, but inside I'm yelling at myself for not being able to keep it clean on my own.

When we're upset with someone, it's a good idea to ask ourselves if the root cause is an expectation that hasn't been met. The next question is whether that expectation was both reasonable and well-communicated to the person involved. If all answers are "yes," then it's probably time to have a talk with the other person or people involved to get their perspective on why your request hasn't been honored. If, on the other hand, the root cause of your anger is an expectation that is either unreasonable or hasn't been clearly communicated, then it is up to you to make the needed adjustment.

What has most upset you lately? Are any of your own expectations at the root of your anger and frustration? Have those expectations been clearly communicated by you? If not, what can you do today to repair that breakdown in communication?

4 FORGIVENESS

… and forgive us our debts, as we also have forgiven our debtors.

Matthew 6:12

During the decluttering process, the toughest items for me have been the ones I inherited from my paternal grandmother, Grannie. I loved her dearly. She was an amazing cook. I have such fond memories of going to their house for holidays and other big meals, watching football games in the fall while eating her delicious chili (with added sausage), and spending the night in order to get up early and see the hot air balloons at Point Mallard on Memorial Day. She was loving, kind, and extremely quick-witted, famously earning all A's when she returned to school for a college degree after raising two boys.

By the end of her life, though, I had built up a resentment against her. From my point of view, she had become self-focused, and it was difficult for me to be around her. I still loved her, but she wasn't the same person she had been when I was younger.

My Granddaddy died suddenly in a fishing accident at

the age of 72, and she never recovered. Of course I expected her to mourn for a long time, but she never managed to move forward with her life even though she lived for an additional fourteen years. She appeared to get ensnared by a great deal of bitterness.

Four years after my Granddaddy's death, my parents sold their house, their business, and most of their belongings to move to Ecuador as missionaries. While this should have been a point of pride for my Grannie, she apparently felt like they were abandoning her and made them feel quite guilty for leaving. At the time, she was in good health. She was financially well-off. She was still living in the same town as most of her closest friends and was perfectly capable of taking care of herself.

But in her mind, she was helpless.

I had expectations of how a Christ-follower was *supposed* to handle losing a spouse. Of course, deep mourning was expected. Obviously, Granddaddy would never be forgotten. But I did expect her to gradually move on with her life in the sense of returning to happiness and independence. From my vantage point, her life did not reflect the great faith that she claimed.

I was so angry with her. I was also defensive. While my parents handled it well, I couldn't stand knowing that either of them felt guilty for leaving her to serve the Lord in another country. How could she put that burden on them? Why couldn't she encourage them in this pursuit of obedience to God's calling?

I never talked with her about this, so I don't have any way of knowing what was truly going on in her mind. It's possible that I was very wrong about her feelings and intentions. Regardless, I was left with a load of disappointment, resentment, and even fear that I needed to confront. Not only was I let down by her not meeting my expectations, I was also frightened by the prospect of some day following in her footsteps. I had often been compared to her in positive ways. Would I react in the same negative ways if I lost my husband? The thought terrified me. I have many of her same tendencies. Was it even possible to reach the end of life walking with the Lord in the way that I had envisioned?

Forgiveness sometimes involves removing reminders

After her death, I inherited some of her possessions. I chose a sterling mirror that had always been on the dresser in the bedroom where I spent the night. I also got a Tiffany-style lamp. My sister and I split her voluminous costume jewelry collection. Years earlier, long before my Granddaddy's death, she had found and restored an antique sideboard. Eventually, she had given it to my parents, and I had gotten it when they moved to Ecuador.

Grannie had three diamond rings – two solitaires and one five-stone anniversary band. Without fully understanding its significance at the time, I chose the anniversary band after her death. My sister and cousin got the other two rings. I later realized that the five diamonds represented five decades and had been given to Grannie by Granddaddy on their 50th wedding anniversary, a little over a year before his death.

As I began to remove more and more things from my home, I had to confront the fact that, when I looked at items around the house that had belonged to her, I had such a conflict of emotions. Seeing them would bring up old feelings of anger followed immediately by guilt over still feeling angry all these years later. It was my deepest desire to be able to forgive her and move on, but those items seemed to always bring up the bad memories instead of the good ones.

I begged God for His help in forgiving her. I so wanted to be free from the emotions and entanglements of anger and bitterness. Yet, no matter what I did, those old feelings seemed to continually rise up when I thought about her.

After much deliberation, I parted with most of the items in my house that had belonged to her. The mirror was only collecting dust and bad feelings on top of my chest of drawers. I had never really liked the colors of the lamp, and the bulb glared jarringly underneath, so it went, too. Some of the earrings and bracelets stayed, but many of those also joined the mirror and lamp in the donate pile. I haven't yet decided about the sideboard, but I believe I would eventually like to replace it with a china hutch.

The ring, of course, stayed. In fact, I wear it every day. Somehow, it never brings up bad memories. I think maybe that's because it pre-dates the negative memories. It's a visible reminder of how much my grandparents loved each other and the longevity of their marriage.

Forgiveness is a process

I have finally been able to move forward in my feelings toward my Grannie. In a strange way, simply thinking about her less has helped. Instead of being reminded of the anger and guilt that I had been carrying every time I walked past her lamp, I now walk past a different lamp that I love. When I wear any of the remaining earrings, they bring back the good memories. And on those (few) days when my husband is getting on my very last nerve, I can glance down at the anniversary ring, realize we're not yet across the second diamond, and recommit to going the full distance with him.

I think perhaps there are two kinds of forgiveness. One type happens instantly and never has to be revisited. You forgive, you move on, you forget about it. That's what I kept searching for with Grannie.

Another type is a longer process. It's a choice that has to continually be made. You forgive, you move on, you remember, and then you forgive again. That's how it has been for me in my feelings toward Grannie. I want it to be over and done, but somehow it hasn't been that simple. And I think having things around that bring up bad memories has just prolonged the process. Maybe someday it will be simply "forgive and move on." Or maybe it will be "forgive ... move on ... (after increasingly long periods) remember ... forgive." Either way, I'm glad to finally be making progress.

Physically removing those items from my house resulted in the removal of burdens to a degree I did not anticipate. I don't think I had really believed in mental, emotional, and spiritual clutter before that point. But I finally found freedom that had been elusive for years.

What about you? Are there people from your past (or even your present) that you have found extremely difficult to forgive? If so, are there items around your house that serve as constant reminders of those negative situations? What clutter needs to go to make room for forgiveness and freedom?

5 LEGACY

After all our hopes and dreams have come and gone
And our children sift through all we've left behind,
May the clues that they discover and the memories they uncover
Become the light that leads them to the road we each must find.

Oh may all who come behind us find us faithful.
May the fire of our devotion light their way.
May the footprints that we leave lead them to believe
And the lives we live inspire them to obey.
  -- *Find Us Faithful* by Steve Green

As I write this, my maternal step-grandmother is unconscious in the hospital being treated for a very serious brain bleed. Her survival is not at all guaranteed. Not only is a brain bleed a huge deal, but she also has other complicating health issues. Although I'm of course praying for her to be healed, I'm not really praying for that on her behalf but on behalf of her family and friends. I have no doubt that whenever Grandmother June leaves this world, she will see Jesus face-to-face. Her faith is evident to all who know her. I've never known anyone else who so embodies the phrase "a gentle and quiet spirit." She will leave behind a legacy of faith.

None of us particularly like to consider our own mortality, but it can be healthy to do so, at least in reasonable doses. While certainly not at the top of the list, one of my motivations for decluttering our massive amount of stuff came from imagining my children having to sort through it after I am gone. It will still be a huge job because I haven't exactly become a minimalist, but at least what is left is actually useful and/or important to me.

May all who come behind us find us faithful (and find what they need)

My parents moved to Ecuador in 2003 to become full-time missionaries. My siblings and I were already grown and married. Although they ended up returning home after four years, the original plan was to be on the field for at least twelve years, so they sold my Dad's veterinary practice along with their home and a large number of their possessions. Before they could actually be sent to the mission field, they were required to tie up loose ends at home, much like when a person is sent off into a war zone for the military. They updated their will, purchased burial plots, and signed over power of attorney for their financial matters and investments. My siblings and I were given information regarding whom to contact if something happened to them. Their financial advisor would know the location of all needed documents and could walk us through the process of settling their estate.

I came across that advisor's business card while decluttering our papers. While I hope it is many more years before I have need to contact him, it's reassuring to know that I have the necessary information. My parents and I should probably exchange house keys, too. I've never dealt with the loss of anyone closer than a grandparent, but I'm certain it's not a time when I would want to be dealing with a locksmith. Emotional pain is unavoidable, but frustration over practical matters can be lessened greatly with a bit of preparation.

While my husband and I have much less in the way of worldly possessions or net worth, I still want to know that my children and other family members could easily locate needed documents. I would not want them to face the added stress of having to deal with boxes and boxes of random papers, not knowing what was important and what was useless. (The life insurance information is in a yellow binder behind my desk. Other key documents are in a file folder marked, prosaically, "Documents.")

Granddaddy's Bible

More than the location of my birth certificate and life insurance policy, I want those left behind to know where I am spending eternity. I want to leave behind a legacy of faith that is clearly seen by those left behind. As it says in the song quoted above, I want the footsteps that I leave to lead them to believe.

So how is that related to decluttering? Well, it means that not only do I want to clear any junk out of my house, I also want to clear any junk out of my life. Just as I choose objects based on whether or not they spark joy for me, I should choose activities and pursuits based on whether or not they spark joy for the Lord. I want to always talk about my faith, not in a forced way but just as a natural consequence of living life in close connection with my children. My kids will no doubt have many memories of me that I could not have anticipated, and certainly some that I would not have deliberately chosen, but I hope they will remember me as someone who loved the Lord and believed His word to be absolutely true and worthy of deep study. I may not be described by them as having a "gentle and quiet spirit," but I want to leave behind a legacy of faith.

My paternal Granddaddy passed away back in 1997. After my Grannie passed away fourteen years later, some of his things were also distributed among family members. I chose his Bible. He was a very wise and Godly man, so I felt that would be the best physical object to represent him. I didn't realize how appropriate it was until I looked through it later. Although it was all clearly well-worn, almost the entire book of Proverbs was highlighted or underlined. His life had exemplified prudence and financial acumen, and this was clearly the source. Although he and Grannie had never had a lot of income during their lives, he had managed it so well that Grannie had more than enough to live very comfortably after he was gone. Obviously, he had not only been a hearer of the Word but a doer as well.

Finishing Strong

Since writing the beginning of this chapter, my step-grandmother June has passed away. While I knew that she was a godly woman who was spiritually prepared for death, I didn't realize how *practically* she was ready. Her own preparations have made this time so much less stressful on her family, especially her husband, children, and grandchildren.

June had two heart surgeries – one in 1997 and the other in 2007. While going through some of her things after her passing, June's daughter found her Bible, and inside were three letters – one to my Granddaddy, and one to each of her two children – written in 2001. She also discovered a list of June's favorite Bible verses and songs to be sung at her funeral. At the time of her death, her home was completely organized and had a freezer full of up-to-date, carefully-labeled meals.

One might suppose that a person so thoughtful about their own mortality might be morbid or depressed. Nothing could have been further from the truth. The week before she died, she was still checking up with friends for whom she was praying. On the day she suffered the brain bleed, she had prepared my Granddaddy's favorite soup for lunch and had spent the afternoon with her daughter and her daughter's family. She was ready to go, in every possible way, and exuded the true "peace that passes all understanding."

I typed the song lyrics at the beginning of this chapter long before any of this happened with my grandmother. My goal had been to encourage others to remain faithful in all seasons of life – even old age – because I hadn't yet witnessed it up close. My Grannie had disappointed me, as I wrote in the last chapter. I didn't know that I was witnessing exactly what I had longed to see because Finishing Strong isn't always something outwardly heroic. June didn't talk about trusting God in spite of major health problems – although that's exactly what she was doing. She just continued walking with Him – nothing more, nothing less, nothing else.

How fitting that *Find Us Faithful* was sung at her funeral.

6 THE PAST MAY EXPLAIN BUT IT DOESN'T DEFINE

Or do you not know that the unrighteous will not inherit the kingdom of God? Do not be deceived: neither the sexually immoral, nor idolaters, nor adulterers, nor men who practice homosexuality, nor thieves, nor the greedy, nor drunkards, nor revilers, nor swindlers will inherit the kingdom of God. <u>And such were some of you.</u> But you were washed, you were sanctified, you were justified in the name of the Lord Jesus Christ and by the Spirit of our God.

1 Corinthians 6:9 - 11 (emphasis mine)

I love the beginning of that last verse: "and such were some of you." We all have things, experiences, even people in our past that we may wish to forget. Perhaps if we could go back in time, we would rewrite entire portions of our history. Notice the next word, though: "but." In Christ, we have been washed clean, sanctified by His blood, and justified by His death and resurrection. We *were*, but now we *are*.

Unearthing memories

I applied the techniques of *The Life-Changing Magic of Tidying Up* by Marie Kondo in my decluttering project. This meant that I followed her directions of decluttering by category instead of location and following a certain order: clothes, books, papers, *komono* (miscellaneous), and sentimental items. While time-consuming, most of the process didn't involve much emotional angst. It was a fairly cerebral activity – just my cup of tea.

But then it was time to deal with the tough stuff.

At first, the boxes of pictures, letters, souvenirs, and so forth weren't nearly as difficult to tackle as I had feared. Lots of great memories came flooding back. While sometimes there were feelings of, "Oh, how little he was back then!" and "How has she grown up so fast?" it wasn't really sad. I found pictures from our honeymoon, from the various places we've lived since we got married seventeen years ago, and from lots of trips my husband and I had taken together as a couple.

Gradually, though, I got deeper into the past. There was the summer I had spent traveling the US and Bulgaria with the Celebrant Singers. There were the high school years. There were pictures from Space Camp when I was convinced that NASA would be a critical part of my future.

Then there were the Acne Years. I had begun to develop severe acne in third grade, and it lasted through about the middle of seventh grade. This had a profound impact on my self-image and self-esteem. There were deep wounds that had been covered over for years but never actually healed. The scars weren't just on my face but also on my psyche. Seeing those pictures in old yearbooks brought back all of those painful memories.

I wrestled with whether or not to keep them. Part of me wanted to throw them away as quickly as possible and as far away as possible. But on the other hand, I knew they might be invaluable if either of my children were to go through the same thing. No one in my life had really known what I felt, and it might have been so helpful to talk with someone who truly understood. In the end, I decided to keep them.

Processing how life has changed over the years

For many years of my life, my number one goal was to become an astronaut. I didn't just attend Space Camp on a whim. I read everything I could get my hands on about the space program, astrophysics, NASA – you name it. I remember reading Carl Sagan's *Cosmos* in junior high school even though I actually understood very little of it.

During a high school Christian youth camp, the speaker had encouraged the attendees to get alone with the Lord and ask Him what was on the throne of our hearts. While many of my friends practically glowed telling how they had been shown crosses and other reassuring things, I had seen one very clear image: a space shuttle. I felt that the Lord wanted me to surrender that dream to Him, and I did so. From that day forward, I never again pursued a career in the space program or any related field.

A while later, I felt called into international missions, and I threw myself wholeheartedly into that pursuit. Not knowing anything else to do on the mission field besides teaching, I volunteered as a Conversational English teacher at my church while pursuing a degree in math. While cleaning out my hope chest, I came across a letter from Russia that had been a response to something I had written. It was from some sort of ministry encouraging me and inviting me to join them in their work. I have no idea now why I never pursued that further or if I tried and nothing came of it.

Somehow in the years between then and now, I had gone from a full-time college math professor to a stay-at-home-mom to a homeschool mom. How did I get from that Point A to my current Point B? What were the intersections along the way, and had I made a wrong turn somewhere? Or were those other things just points along the journey God had laid out for me all along? Clearly, marrying David had been perhaps the most critical juncture in my life. Had I married the wrong person?

How had my life goals changed from Astronaut to Missionary to Homeschool Mom? Had I somehow missed God's calling, or was I right where He wanted me to be? My life was very different from what I had expected back then. How did that happen? And was it a good thing?

While there is some value to be gained from asking these questions, at the end of the day, it's a moot point. I do happen to believe that I married the right man – I can't imagine anyone better suited for me – but it may be impossible for me to actually know for sure in an empirical sense. However, I do know for sure that it is God's will for me to stay married to him. I can't go back in time and change any of the decisions that I made. They have all shaped me into the person that I am now. The only valid question is this: who am I now, and where do I go from here?

Saying what needs to be said – to others and to myself

When I look in the mirror now, I like what I see. I finally feel beautiful. While that girl with the horrible acne sometimes still peeks out from behind those eyes, her image fades with each passing year. And again I find myself asking, "How did I get from that Point A (feeling ugly and wishing to be invisible most of the time) to this Point B (finally feeling confident in my appearance and abilities)?" While certainly the Lord must receive the greatest credit in this, His work in my life was often embodied in my husband. I sometimes joke that I married my husband because he liked my legs. It's not entirely untrue. He saw me as a beautiful woman, and he was so convincing that I started to believe it, too.

Before knowing David, my life was consumed with making other people happy. I was even consumed with trying to make God happy, although I didn't really see it that way at the time. He helped to set me free from that hamster wheel of performance. He helped me to learn that I was capable of making decisions for myself. He loved me when I succeeded and when I faltered. He loved me with makeup and without it. He laughed at my jokes and delighted in my secret dreams.

Considering why we made various choices over the years can be very instructive and revealing. But the past does not define us. It doesn't limit us and what we are capable of doing from this point forward.

However, the past can give us insight into the ways God has prepared us not only for our current circumstances but also for the future He has in store for us. As someone once said to me, nothing is ever wasted in God's economy. To gain insight into how God may be wanting to use me now, it can be very instructive to look back at how He has used me most effectively in the past. That thirst for knowledge that appeared in reading all of those space books is what continues to make me a productive researcher and analyst of various options. The lessons learned from teaching English to non-native speakers and from struggling through graduate school have made me a much more effective teacher. Years spent under the leadership of various Bible teachers have enabled me to have insights to share with other young wives and mothers.

No, the past doesn't define us, and it doesn't always explain our current situation, but there is much to be gleaned from the lessons it contains.

7 FIND FREEDOM IN BEING WHO GOD CREATED YOU TO BE

When a room becomes cluttered, the cause is more than just physical. Visible mess helps distract us from the true source of the disorder. The act of cluttering is really an instinctive reflex that draws our attention away from the heart of an issue. If you can't feel relaxed in a clean and tidy room, try confronting your feeling of anxiety. It may shed light on what is really bothering you. When your room is clean and uncluttered, you have no choice but to examine your inner state. You can see any issues you have been avoiding and are forced to deal with them. From the moment you start tidying, you will be compelled to reset your life.

-- Marie Kondo, *The Life-Changing Magic of Tidying Up*

When I turned forty, I suddenly found clarity and courage in ways I hadn't experienced before. It started where many true transformations begin – in a hair salon. Instead of just getting my usual blonde highlights and a trim, I suggested maybe trying something a bit different: pink. Not only that, I wanted the rest of my hair to be darker. I emerged, just a few days shy of my birthday, looking completely different. I no longer blended in to the background. I couldn't blend in any more. I had bright pink highlights in dark brown hair.

The next morning was the first test of my new look. It was homeschool co-op day. Not only would I be out in public, I'd be around other very conservative homeschool moms. I didn't expect anyone to be rude, but I wasn't sure what else to expect. Surprisingly, many were quite complimentary, and some even seemed a bit envious.

The toughest place was actually the grocery store. Older ladies did little to hide their disapproval. I could tell they were making judgements about me in their minds. I knew that's what was going on because it's what would have been going on in my mind, too. I'm sure they were imagining the various tattoos and piercings I must surely have and the type of music I must listen to. Their assumptions could not have been further from the truth.

On the other hand, though, my hair opened conversations with people who likely would have not spoken to me before precisely because of their assumptions about my usual look. Suddenly those tattooed, pierced, hair-dyed people were asking me questions about my hair. Instead of assuming that I was ultra-conservative and standoffish, they thought of me as one of their own. They, also, were wrong.

Turns out, the true Laura is somewhere in the middle.

A Laura House

I am blessed to have a good relationship with my mother. Sure, we have occasional disagreements, and sometimes we drive each other nuts, but we generally have a truly mutual respect for one another. I know that she is my biggest fan.

She's said many encouraging words and kind

compliments to me over the years, but my very favorite is this: when she came into my house most recently (having not been inside since we had painted several more rooms, decluttered bags upon bags of stuff, and done a bit of redecorating), she declared, "Ahh, now this is a Laura House!" She could see evidence of my personality everywhere. My outer world had become a reflection of my inner self.

Obviously, if you're married and/or have children, your husband and children should be considered in making decisions about the look of your home. But I believe that the woman of the house sets the tone, and that even includes the physical feel of the house. Our walls have pictures of times, places, words, and especially people that bring a smile to my face. The colors chosen brighten my spirit. We didn't build the house, so there are certainly parts that aren't to my taste and are beyond our budget to change, but I've changed what I can to focus on the parts of the house that I enjoy.

Don't be afraid to take risks. If you have always followed someone else's recommendations for your home, branch out and try something different. In Marie Kondo's book (quoted above), her standard for deciding what to keep is to ask, "Does it spark joy?" I think that applies to paint colors and furniture, too.

If you're renting, the choices may be quite a bit more limited, but even there, joy can be added. What's your favorite color? Find some curtains or throw pillows in that shade. Think about your five senses. How can you add sights, sounds, smells, textures, and tastes that you love to your environment?

Not sure what you really like? I understand. Once you've fully decluttered, though, take a look at the things you have chosen to keep. Is there a common theme in your books? Is there a color scheme emerging from your closet? Did you hold on to your pasta maker but eschew your chopsticks? These are all important clues.

Passing on the Hope Chest

When I was eighteen years old, my parents bought me a hope chest for Christmas. It was a high-quality piece of furniture, cedar-lined to protect valuables inside. I had begun collecting pieces of Christmas china a few years earlier, and this gave me a good place to store any new pieces. It also became the resting place for lots of high school and early-college memorabilia. When my parents sold the house where I had spent part of my growing-up years and couldn't store it any longer, it became a part of my furnishings.

I tried to make it work. It lived at the foot of our bed for a while. It was in the living room in another house. When we moved to our current house, it had ended up inside my husband's closet.

Truthfully, it just wasn't "me." The top was covered with cushioned fabric that depicted a boy and girl holding hands in a pastoral scene with a church in the background. Think: Little House on the Prairie meets Precious Moments. Now, I love Little House – the show and the books – and at one time I also liked Precious Moments figurines, but my decorating style – albeit a bit eclectic – definitely isn't "country."

The first time I said out-loud to my husband, "I'm thinking of getting rid of my hope chest," I felt like I was contemplating some sort of treason. My parents had given it to me. I'd had it for many years. It was a very sturdy piece of furniture. But it was very out of place in my home.

Before passing it on, I talked it over with my daughter. I explained what it was, where it had originated, and how it would eventually be passed on to her if I kept it. I asked her to be completely honest with me and asked if she wanted it. At first, she hesitantly said, "I guess so." But after reassuring her that I really did want her honest opinion, she said that she didn't want it. She said, "Maybe if the top was more … 'new-timey'…" (as opposed to old-timey). I knew exactly what she meant.

Fortunately, I have one niece in particular who loves just that sort of style. She absolutely adores the chest. So now it's in her parents' attic until she is older. It's being loved. It's still in the family. But it's no longer in my house – the Laura House.

Is your house a (Your Name) House? If so, what makes it that way, and can you spread that general "feel" to other areas of your life? If not, what small change could you make today to move in that direction?

8 MOVING FORWARD

When you choose to have a Sabbath heart about your activities
and possessions, you're doing more than just keeping yourself
from living a stress-filled, clutter-laden life. You are also
honoring God's purpose by setting aside space and time to foster
holy intimacy.
-- Priscilla Shirer, *Breathe*

I began this book with a discussion of the Sabbath principle as it applied to decluttering. The Sabbath command – the command to abstain from the work that had become such a constant in the lives of the Israelites during their captivity in Egypt – was crucial in changing a mindset bent toward the constant need to appease the gods and slave masters under whose rule they had existed. For two years, God continued to declutter the minds and hearts of the people as they learned to follow Him, obey His much different commands, and receive His daily provision of manna to eat.

At the end of those first two years, the people faced their first major test of faith. Had their minds and hearts really been changed or only their location? They stood at the entrance to the Promised Land, the area that had been promised to the Israelites when God spoke to Abraham many years before the birth of Isaac. Twelve men had spent forty days exploring this new land. It was everything God had promised. The land was productive. Food was abundant. But it wasn't uninhabited. Some action – some very real risk – was required to move into the land.

Two years is not a very long time. Just two years prior, they had witnessed the plagues in Egypt. Just two years earlier, they had walked across dry land with walls of Red Sea on either side of them. Every day they had seen the column of cloud in the sky, and every night they had seen the column of fire. They had followed the cloud. They had eaten the manna.

For two years, they had experienced true rest. They were no longer working to complete exhaustion day after day in fear for their lives. The bar was not continually being reset in a higher groove.

Up until now, they had seen and then trusted. The waters parted before they moved forward. They had a visible image of cloud and fire to follow. The manna fell during the night, and they gathered it in the morning. Now, would they trust what they had not yet seen?

With the exception of two of the spies, Joshua and Caleb, the answer was no.

> *And all the people of Israel grumbled against Moses and Aaron. The whole congregation said to them, "Would that we had died in the land of Egypt! Or would that we had died in this wilderness! Why is the Lord bringing us into this land, to fall by the sword? Our wives and our little ones will become a prey. Would it not be better for us to go back to Egypt?" And they said to one another, "Let us choose a leader and go back to Egypt."* Numbers 14: 2 – 4

They wanted to go back to Egypt. The people

preferred captivity to risk. They were asking for coercion instead of rest. Their minds and hearts had not really been changed, only their location. It would take another forty years of desert wandering before they would be ready to enter the Promised Land.

In some ways, decluttering our homes is not unlike the Israelites leaving Egypt and spending those first two years headed toward Canaan. Some parts of the process will feel monumental, like walking across the Red Sea on dry land. Other parts will feel like drudgery, like packing up a tent every so often to move on to a new location. Some of it will just be ordinary, like a typical Tuesday in a mid-desert campground. But hopefully, by both big leaps and tiny steps, our mindsets will be altered. By the time the task is completed, our location should have changed – our surroundings should be noticeably different from where we began. Hopefully our minds will be changed as well.

Kind of like a diet, beginning is very difficult. Continuing is even harder. But the most challenging part of all comes after the goal has been reached – maintaining. After the last load of clutter has been donated to the thrift store and the space is wonderfully organized, how will that state be maintained? Once schedules have been tamed and old sin patterns have been erased, how will they stay that way? How can we move forward and not "choose a leader and go back to Egypt?"

I'd like to suggest two steps:

1. Remember

When the Israelites finally crossed over the Jordan River into the Promised Land, the first thing they did was to set up a visual reminder for themselves and for their descendants.

> ... *take twelve stones from here out of the midst of the Jordan, from the very place where the priests' feet stood firmly, and bring them over with you ... that this may be a sign among you.*

When your children ask in time to come, "What do those stones mean to you" then you shall tell them that the waters of the Jordan were cut off before the ark of the covenant of the Lord. When it passed over the Jordan, the waters of the Jordan were cut off. So these stones shall be to the people of Israel a memorial forever. Joshua 4: 3, 6-7

Hopefully you took some "before" pictures before beginning your decluttering journey. If so, I recommend looking at them periodically to remind yourself of how things used to be. If you don't have pictures – and perhaps even if you do – I would suggest writing about how you felt trapped in all of that clutter. It doesn't have to be beautiful prose. This is only for you.

For the mental, emotional, and spiritual clutter that you have tossed, try doing the same thing. Take time to remember how it felt to have a life clogged up with too many activities, unforgiveness, people-pleasing, and sinful habits. Don't let this exercise bring any guilt back, though. The purpose is to remember how far you've come, not how far away you had gone.

2. Repeat

Periodically, go through the decluttering process again. I'm in the middle of doing that right now myself, and it has been a wonderful way to refocus. I haven't actually gotten rid of anything else, but it's been very beneficial to look at items and ask, "Do I still want this? Am I still happy having this around my house?" It has only taken me a few minutes per room or category because the hard work is already complete. This is just a check-up.

As before, apply this to other non-physical aspects of your life. Have you taken on too much lately? Have you drifted away from the Lord over the last few weeks or months? What can you do to get back on track today?

Perfection is impossible, but maintenance is not. You will sometimes buy more than you need or want. You will occasionally take on more commitments than you can healthily manage. Your relationship with the Lord may lose its fire from time to time. The key is to make sure this is only a temporary condition. Don't go back into clutter, busyness, and complacency. Don't go back into slavery. Don't return to Egypt. Maintain a Sabbath-margined home, calendar, and heart. Remain free.

WHAT WORKED FOR ME

Although this book is not about how to declutter, I know many of you are like me and really want to know what has worked for someone else. I have tried many different methods. Most boiled down to the 15-minutes-a-day approach of FlyLady and the Sidetracked Home Executives. I don't doubt that that approach can and does work for many people. It just didn't ever work for me.

The process that finally worked for me was what I found in the book *The Life-Changing Magic of Tidying Up* by Marie Kondo. Even though her personality and approach are, at best, a little … different, I think it was this very difference that finally clicked for me. Two basic ideas make it distinct from other approaches: 1. Finish "tidying" (decluttering) your entire home as quickly as possible – preferably within a six-month timespan, and 2. Make decisions about whether to keep or toss an item based on your emotional reaction to it – "Does it spark joy?"

The logical, "thinking" part of my brain is usually going ninety miles an hour. I have a hard time making decisions because I can almost always justify or rationalize either choice. As a result of all of this thinking, it's sometimes very difficult for me to hear my emotions or my gut instinct. Marie Kondo's approach forced me to get past my head and let my heart make some decisions. This was incredibly freeing. I no longer had to prove logically that something should be kept or should be tossed. If I loved it, it stayed. If I didn't, it was gone.

Again, this book that you are reading right now is not a how-to book, so feel free to follow whatever path works for you. But if you haven't yet found an approach that works, and especially if you get stuck in your head like I do, you might want to give Marie's book a try.

STUDY GUIDE

I have developed a 5-week Bible study that goes along with this book. It is suitable for individual or group study. If you would like to know more about the study or would like to purchase a copy, please contact me at we4baggetts@gmail.com.

WORKS CITED
AND
RECOMMENDED READING

Brueggemann, W. (2014). *Sabbath as Resistance: Saying No to the Culture of Now.* Louisville: Westminster John Knox Press.

Buchanan, M. (2006). *The Rest of God: Restoring Your Soul by Restoring Sabbath.* Nashville: Thomas Nelson.

Chastek, J. (2010, July 13). *Our ecclesiastical, social, and cultural abandonment of self-denial.* Retrieved from Just Thomism: https://thomism.wordpress.com/2010/07/13/our-ecclesiastic-social-and-cultural-abandonment-of-self-denial/

Kondo, M. (2014). *The Life-Changing Magic of Tidying Up: The Japanese Art of Decluttering and Organizing.* New York: Ten Speed Press.

Shirer, P. (2015). *Breathe: Making Room for Sabbath.* Nashville: Lifeway Press.

ABOUT THE AUTHOR

Raised to be a career girl, Laura Baggett learned that God had other plans. She is a college math instructor who is learning to teach elementary school at home with her two favorite students. She and her husband have moved 13 times during their 18 years of marriage, learning to live out the phrase "Bloom Where You're Planted."

As a writer and teacher, her purpose is to illuminate and communicate Biblical principles to believers – especially wives and mothers – so they can assimilate the Word of God and eliminate mental, emotional, spiritual, and physical clutter from their lives.

How to connect with me:

I would love to hear from you. The best places to find me are on Facebook (www.facebook.com/LauraBaggett) or via e-mail at we4baggetts@gmail.com

94056246R00033

Made in the USA
Lexington, KY
22 July 2018